THE BIG 5: AFRICAN SAFARI ANIMALS

LEOPARD

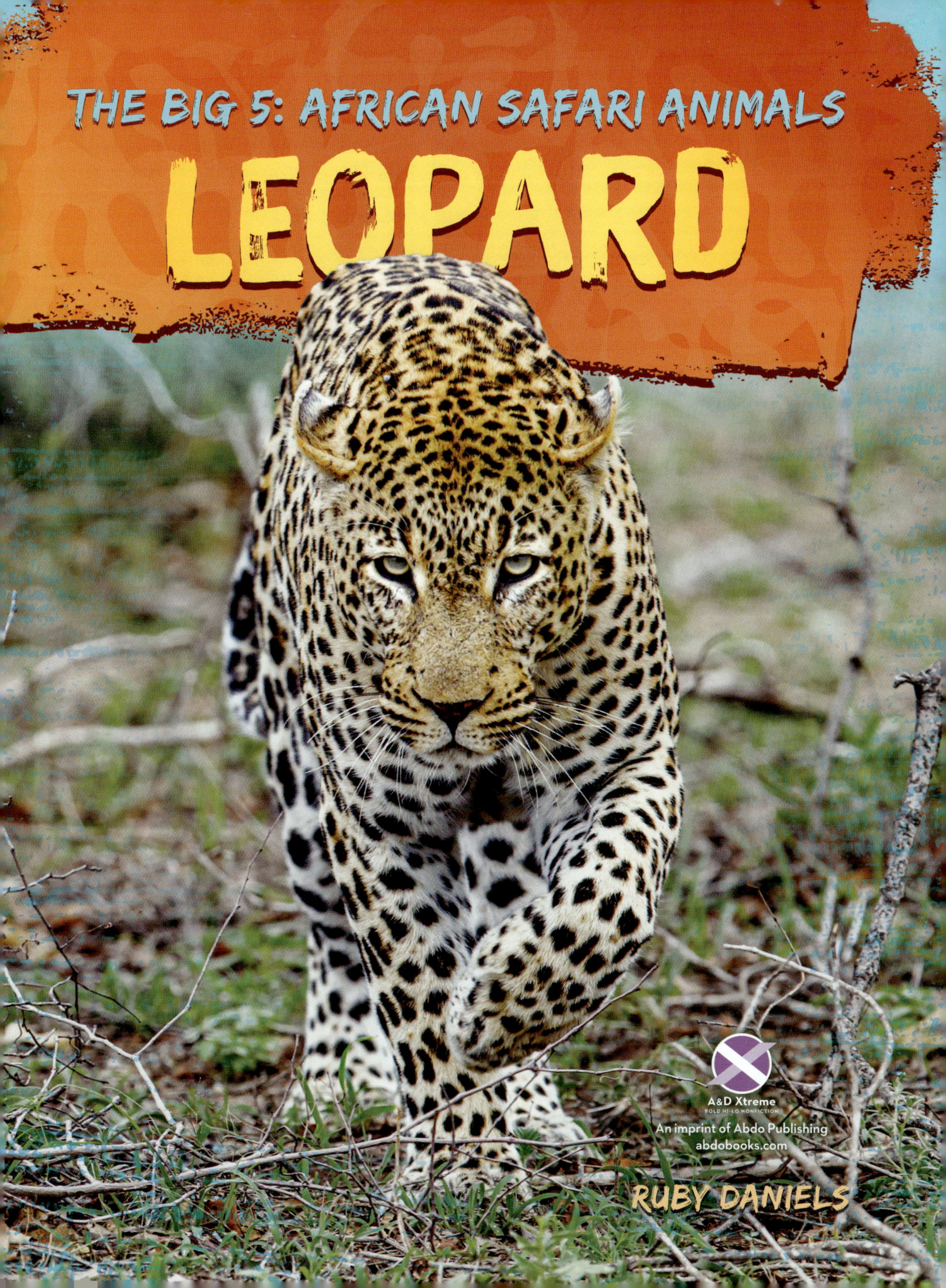

A&D Xtreme
BOLD HI-LO NONFICTION
An imprint of Abdo Publishing
abdobooks.com

RUBY DANIELS

TAKE IT TO THE XTREME!

GET READY FOR AN EXTREME ADVENTURE! THE PAGES OF THIS BOOK WILL TAKE YOU INTO THE THRILLING WORLD OF ICONIC AFRICAN ANIMALS. WHEN YOU HAVE FINISHED READING THIS BOOK, TAKE THE XTREME CHALLENGE ON PAGE 45 ABOUT WHAT YOU'VE LEARNED!

ABDOBOOKS.COM
Published by Abdo Publishing, a division of ABDO, PO Box 398166, Minneapolis, Minnesota 55439.

Printed in the United States of America, North Mankato, MN.
052025
092025

THIS BOOK CONTAINS RECYCLED MATERIALS

Design: Kelly Doudna, Mighty Media, Inc.
Production: Mighty Media, Inc.
Editor: Katherine Chu

Cover Photograph: Ilan Horn/Shutterstock

Interior Photographs: Andrew Mohamed/Shutterstock, pp. 8-9; David Macharia/Shutterstock, pp. 14–15; Heinrich Neumeyer/Shutterstock, pp. 32–33; Henk Bogaard/Shutterstock, pp. 40–41; Ilan Horn/Shutterstock, p. 1; Jeremy Richards/Shutterstock, pp. 38–39; Joefke/Adobe Stock, pp. 34–35; Johan W. Elzenga/Shutterstock, pp. 24–25; Jurgens Potgieter/Shutterstock, pp. 22–23; Katiekk/Shutterstock, pp. 36–37; Lori Labrecque/Adobe Stock, pp. 20–21; Maggy Meyer/Shutterstock, pp. 18–19, 42–43; Martin Mecnarowski/Shutterstock, pp. 26-27; nattanan726/Shutterstock, pp. 6-7; Phillip Allaway/Shutterstock, p. 44; PhotocechCZ/Shutterstock, pp. 30–31; Simone Janssen/Shutterstock, pp. 10-11; Thomas Retterath/Shutterstock, pp. 4-5; Vladimir Turkenich/Shutterstock, pp. 12-13; Wirestock/iStockphoto, pp. 16-17; Wirestock Creators/Shutterstock, pp. 28-29

Design Elements: DGIM studio/Adobe Stock (distressed texture); Ografica/Adobe Stock (header background); Zebra Finch/Adobe Stock (header background)

LIBRARY OF CONGRESS CONTROL NUMBER: 2024948561
PUBLISHER'S CATALOGINGIN-PUBLICATION DATA
Names: Daniels, Ruby, author.
Title: Leopard / by Ruby Daniels
Description: Minneapolis, Minnesota : Abdo Publishing, 2026 | Series: The big 5: African safari animals | Includes online resources and index.
Identifiers: ISBN 9781098296322 (lib. bdg.) | ISBN 9798384917755 (ebook)
Subjects: LCSH: Leopard--Juvenile literature. | Black panther--Juvenile literature. | Big game animals--Africa--Juvenile literature. | Carnivorous animals--Juvenile literature. | Safaris--Juvenile literature.
Classification: DDC 591.96--dc23

CONTENTS

CHAPTER 1

LEOPARD LOUNGE

While on a night safari in Zambia, you hear a rustling sound above you. Your guide shines a light up in the trees. You glimpse a furry tail hanging down. Then you see the beautiful spots and amber eyes of a big cat lying on a branch. You've just spotted a leopard!

Leopards live for up to 12 years in the wild. They can live much longer in zoos.

CHAPTER 2

PART OF THE BIG 5

African leopards are part of a group of African animals called the Big 5. These include Cape buffalo, elephants, leopards, lions, and rhinoceroses.

Originally, the Big 5 got this name because they were the most challenging animals to hunt. But today, they are popular animals for people to view on safaris.

Leopards are good swimmers.

CHAPTER 3

THE AFRICAN LEOPARD

The African leopard is a **subspecies** of leopard. The leopard is smaller than most other big cats. It is about seven feet (2.1 m) long. It stands only about two feet (0.6 m) tall at the shoulder. It weighs up to 200 pounds (90.7 kg).

XTREME FACT

The snow leopard is not actually a leopard. It is more closely related to tigers.

A leopard's tail can be more than three feet (0.9 m) long.

Leopards have yellowish fur with white **bellies**. They are known for their rosettes. Rosettes are the spots that cover their body. Some leopards have black fur and spots. They are known as black panthers.

A leopard's rosettes help it blend in with its surroundings.

XTREME FACT

Leopards in different areas have differently shaped rosettes. Leopards in East Africa have round rosettes. Leopards in southern Africa have square rosettes.

Leopards can leap forward 20 feet (6.1 m) and jump 10 feet (3 m) in the air.

Leopards are very powerful. They have long bodies, short legs, and strong shoulder blades. The leopard is the strongest climber of all big cats. It uses its strength to climb trees.

XTREME FACT

Leopards can run up to 36 miles per hour (58 kmh)!

CHAPTER 4

LIFE ACROSS AFRICA

African leopards live in regions south of the African Sahara Desert and in northeast Africa. They live in different types of **habitats**. These include grasslands, **savannas**, mountains, rainforests, deserts, and more.

Leopards can live anywhere, but prefer dense bush and forests with rivers.

Leopards mark their territory with urine. They also claw and rub against trees.

Leopards are mainly nocturnal. This means they are mostly active at night. Leopards also usually live alone and have their own territory. Males' territories may **overlap** with females' territories. This is how they find each other to mate.

XTREME FACT

Leopards' territories can be more than 700 square miles (1,813 sq km).

A female leopard's **gestation** period lasts about three months. Female leopards carry their cubs until they are old enough to walk. After two or three months, cubs begin to play and learn to hunt. They live with their mother for about two years.

XTREME FACT

Leopard cubs are born with barely visible spots. The spots darken as the cubs grow.

Female leopards have litters of two or three cubs.

XTREME FACT

Leopards communicate through many sounds. They cough, growl, and even purr.

Leopards are **carnivores**. They eat small creatures like fish, birds, and rodents. And they eat larger animals like warthogs, impalas, and baboons. Leopards use **stealth** to hunt their prey. They usually carry their prey up into a tree to eat.

Leopards store their food in tree branches. They do this to hide it from lions and hyenas, who might try to take the food.

CHAPTER 5

LEOPARDS UNDER THREAT

Leopards are **vulnerable**. This means the **species** is at high risk of becoming **extinct** in the wild. There are more African leopards than other leopard **subspecies**. Still, they face many threats. These include other predators, poaching, **habitat** loss and fragmentation, and human-leopard conflict.

There are nine different subspecies of leopard. They live throughout Africa and Asia.

Leopards are apex predators. This means they have no natural predators. But lions and packs of hyenas sometimes hunt and kill leopards. They also compete with leopards for prey.

Poaching is a form of illegal hunting. People poach leopards for their fur to make coats and other items. People also kill leopards for their claws, whiskers, and tails. Some people believe these items have special powers.

Leopards successfully catch about 14 to 38 percent of the prey they hunt.

Other people poach animals such as warthogs for their meat. This is called **bushmeat** hunting. Leopards rely on prey for food. Bushmeat hunting reduces the number of prey animals that leopards can hunt. With less prey, leopards may not have enough to eat. So, they might **starve** or hunt livestock instead.

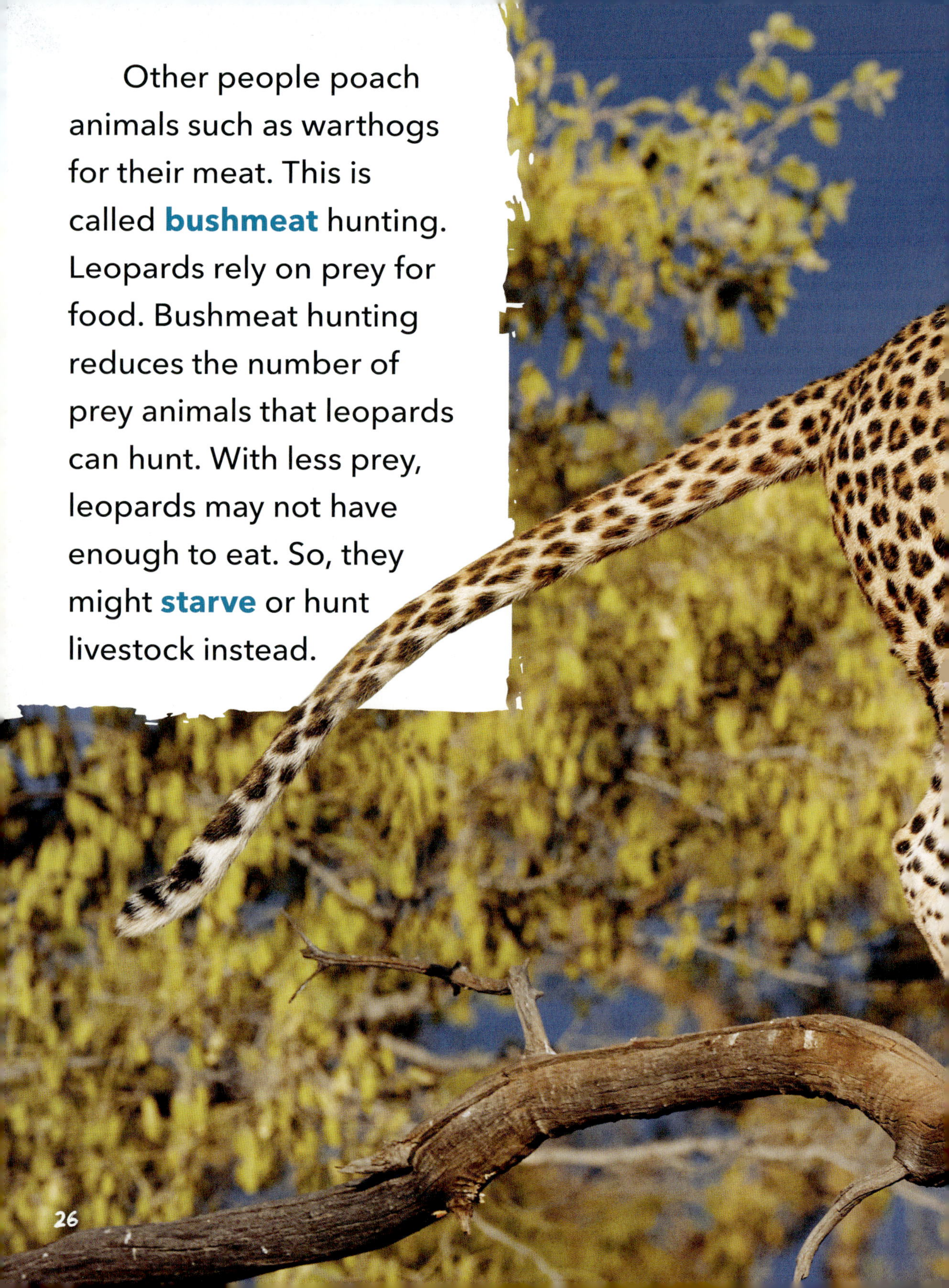

Leopards eat about 880 pounds
(400 kg) of meat each year.

Leopards have lost about 31 percent of their available land around the world due to habitat loss and fragmentation.

Human activity is the main cause of **habitat** loss and fragmentation. Habitat loss is when the size of an animal's habitat is reduced. Habitat fragmentation is when an animal's habitat is broken up. For leopards, reduced or broken up habitats mean less prey.

Human-leopard conflict is another problem that occurs when leopards live near humans. When hungry, leopards may eat livestock. Ranchers sometimes kill leopards in anger or to prevent this from happening.

CHAPTER 6

ESSENTIAL ANIMALS

The loss of African leopards is a serious issue. They are important for the survival of other **species** in their **ecosystem**. Leopards kill other animals. But this helps keep the ecosystem balanced.

Experts believe there are more than 700,000 leopards in Africa, but their numbers are decreasing.

By killing their prey, leopards control the populations of **herbivores**. Without leopards, herbivores would become overpopulated. This means there would be too many herbivores and not enough plants.

Leopards hunt by stalking or using slow movements. This way, they can get close enough to pounce before their prey can run away.

Leopards also keep baboon populations under control. Baboons mostly eat plants. But they also eat small **mammals**, birds, insects, reptiles, and fish. Fewer baboons mean these smaller **species** can flourish.

CHAPTER 7

HELP IS ON THE WAY

Conservationists work hard to protect African leopards. Many organizations create and manage national parks for leopards and other wildlife. These protected areas save wildlife from **habitat** loss and poaching.

Leopards are more active at night and can be hard to find. So, conservationists may use camera traps to track and learn about this animal.

Bomas are walls that keep livestock in and predators out. They can be made from wood, thorny bushes, or wire mesh. The African Wildlife Foundation is helping build better, movable bomas.

Conservationists also try to reduce human-leopard conflict. Ranchers rely on their livestock for income. So, some organizations raise money for ranchers who lose their livestock to predators. And other organizations build better enclosures to protect livestock. Both of these efforts help prevent leopard deaths.

Some organizations use special collars to track and study leopard numbers and activities. **Conservationists** also use the collars to help leopards. For example, the collars can send a signal to conservationists if a leopard has stopped moving for long periods of time. This might mean the leopard is sick or in danger. Conservationists can then help the animal.

Wildlife ACT is an organization working on making a special type of collar that can prevent leopards from choking when caught in a poacher's snare.

CHAPTER 8

FAN FAVORITES

African leopards are popular animals to view on safaris. They are marvelous and have exceptional abilities. People on safari may witness astonishing scenes like leopards hunting or climbing trees.

However, leopards are nocturnal and shy animals. Visitors may need to go on night safaris or go off-road to see a leopard in action.

Leopards have large eyes and wide pupils. This helps them see clearly in the dark.

There are many areas where people can see leopards on safari. Kruger National Park in South Africa and South Luangwa National Park in Zambia both

have high populations of leopards. National parks in Kenya, Botswana, Tanzania, and more also offer great possibilities for leopard viewing.

Lucky safari visitors might get to see leopard cubs play fighting.

CHAPTER 9

MORE TO EXPLORE

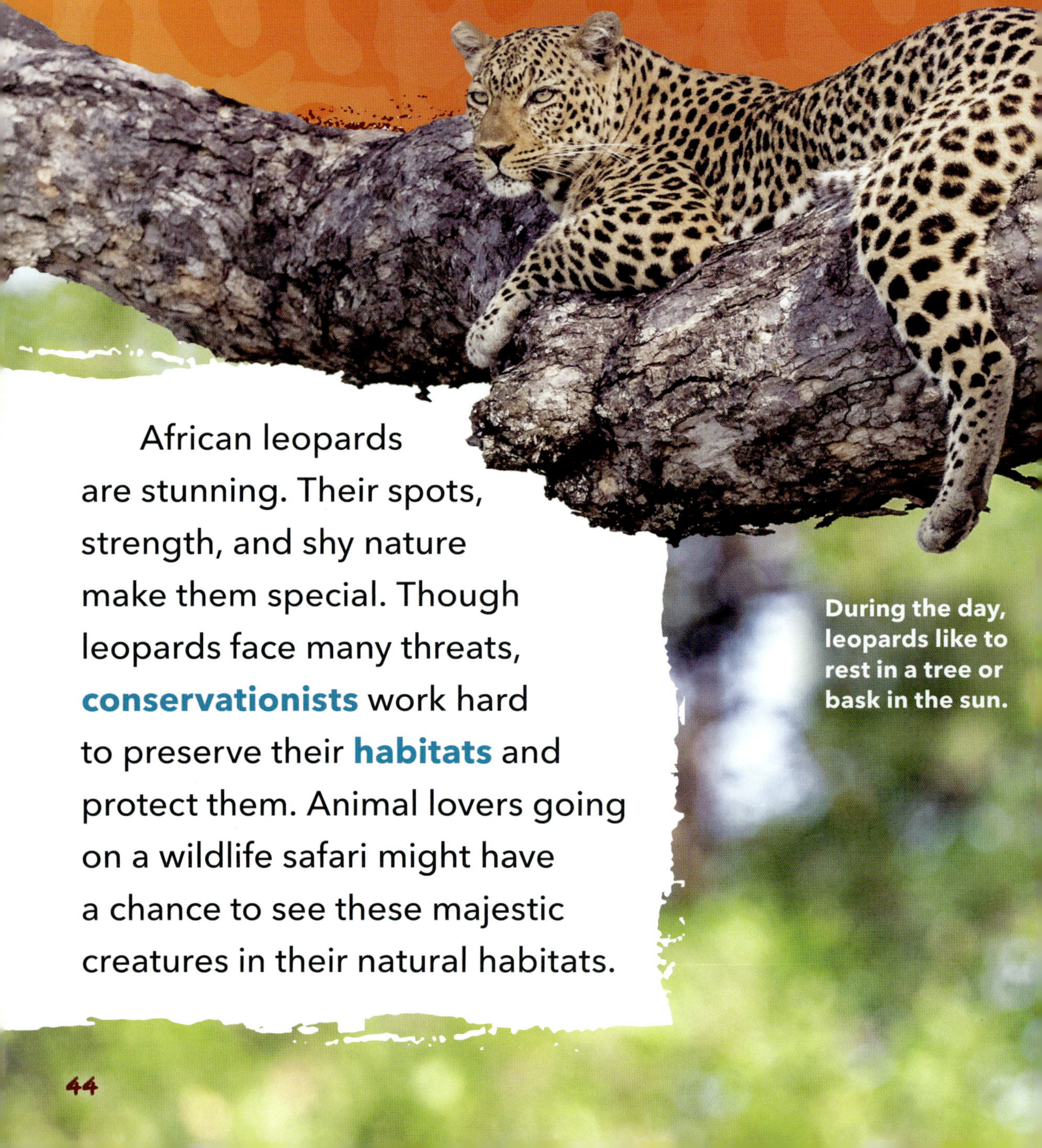

African leopards are stunning. Their spots, strength, and shy nature make them special. Though leopards face many threats, **conservationists** work hard to preserve their **habitats** and protect them. Animal lovers going on a wildlife safari might have a chance to see these majestic creatures in their natural habitats.

During the day, leopards like to rest in a tree or bask in the sun.

XTREME CHALLENGE

TAKE THE QUIZ BELOW AND PUT WHAT YOU'VE LEARNED TO THE TEST!

1) What qualities make leopards special?

2) What type of habitats do leopards live in?

3) How does poaching affect leopards?

4) Why do conservationists place special collars on leopards?

5) Would you want to see leopards on a safari? Why or why not?

GLOSSARY

belly–the underside of an animal's body.

bushmeat–meat that comes from hunting wild animals.

carnivore–an animal that eats meat.

conservation–the planned management of natural resources or animals to protect them from damage or destruction. People who do this are conservationists.

ecosystem–a community of organisms and their surroundings.

extinct–no longer existing.

gestation–the carrying of a developing unborn baby in the uterus.

habitat–a place where a living thing is naturally found.

herbivore–an animal that eats only plants.

mammal–a warm-blooded animal that has hair and whose females produce milk to feed their young.

overlap–to occupy the same area in part.

savanna–a grassy plain with few or no trees.

species–a group of related living beings that can naturally produce offspring with each other.

starve—to suffer or die from lack of food.

stealth—an action or behavior performed in a secretive or sneaky manner.

subspecies—a group of related organisms ranking below a species. Members of a subspecies often share a common geographic range.

vulnerable—able to be hurt or attacked. An animal has a vulnerable status when it is likely to become endangered.

ONLINE RESOURCES

Booklinks
NONFICTION NETWORK
FREE! ONLINE NONFICTION RESOURCES

To learn more about African leopards, please visit **abdobooklinks.com** or scan this QR code. These links are routinely monitored and updated to provide the most current information available.

INDEX